$ell more eBook$

How to increase sales and Amazon rankings
using Kindle Direct Publishing

**By Lucinda Sue Crosby
& Laura Dobbins**

LuckyCinda
http://kindlebookpromos.luckycinda.com

http://kindlebookpromos.luckycinda.com

First Edition August 2012
LuckyCinda Publishing

ISBN-13: 978-1478180029 (CreateSpace-Assigned)
ISBN-10: 1478180021

Cover designed by Laura Dobbins
Image by DreamsTime (http://dreamstime.com)

Copyeditor Ruth Justis

Printed in USA

Contact: www.luckycinda.com

Table of Contents

Introduction

This book will outline how to better manage your hard copy inventory and boost sales through e-publishing. You'll learn:

- How to market your e-books online
- How to navigate Amazon and plan/implement proven selling strategies for the best results
- How to reduce marketing costs and product overhead costs

We'll also cover:

- Kindle Direct Publishing promotions that can improve your Amazon rankings
- KDP's other revenue opportunities
- The art of Free Promotions and how to keep the "Book Buzz" going

Before we get to the innovative stuff, we've outlined some basics and essentials. Of course, every book is unique. The success of your product will depend on its quality, long and short-term marketing methods and whether consumers like it or not. But everyone has the same shot at success.

Why not you?

Here's to your achievements ... Let's get started!

Chapter 1 - Isn't it time you take charge of your future?

If you're an author or writer and you are looking to SELL what you've produced, most of the real work comes AFTER the book exists in the physical universe.

Over the past decade, book publishing and marketing have both been heavily influenced by the galloping growth in print-on-demand and Internet advertising technologies. However, many of the so-called "tried-and-true" book marketing strategies developed since 2000, that worked perfectly well for seven or eight years, are rapidly becoming obsolete. Now that anyone can publish a book, competition to get noticed is more furious than ever. Amazon lists more than 3 million books already in print and over 1 million digital e-books ... with the lists lengthening daily.

You may think landing a deal with a big publishing company is the answer to your prayers. But too many of the largest established literary houses haven't mastered, or even grasped, the revolution that's occurring under their noses. They resist embracing the NEW WORLD of the PRINTED WORD and, therefore, are not actively shaping it.

To be fair, some establishment resistance to Do-It-Yourself Publishing is understandable. After all, the mere ability to produce a book doesn't guarantee that the end result will be commercially viable, no matter how polished the prose.

Currently, traditional publishers work much the same way they have since Charles Dickens penned *A Tale of Two Cities,* except that e-mail inboxes are now the preferred repository for queries and unsolicited manuscripts. Even if your submission rises to the top like cream, it must still undergo a lengthy process before it sees the light of day.

If you sign with a publisher, his or her job is to ensure your labor of love is properly edited, designed, produced, distributed and sold. This requires hundreds, if not thousands, of man-hours depending on the project. Since the costs associated with producing and marketing are expected by publishers to be recovered through sales, literary agencies need to be selective.

About 12 years ago, independent book publishers and marketers began repopulating the literary landscape, some reputable, some not. Frankly, it's not difficult to take advantage of new writers whose only wish is to see their work in print. So it's vital to do your homework whatever publishing route you choose, traditional or otherwise.

Caveat Emptor! One all-too-common mistake for first-time self-publishers: Overstocking. It doesn't make sense to print 1,000 books if you have nobody to sell to after your friends and family buy the first 100. Big-name publishing firms don't usually print more than 5,000 to 10,000 copies unless the author is well-known or the topic controversial enough to generate large sales. For self or independent publishers, we suggest starting with 200 to 500 copies.

A more cost-effective approach is using Print on Demand (POD), which makes it possible for any writer to hold copies of his/her work in hand. In some cases, the cost is less than $3 a book, including shipping. That price point is one reason digital publishing has exploded in popularity with an exponential increase in electronic book sales that require no paper copies at all. When and if you pre-sell traditional-form books, you simply order them.

So far so good, but here's the million dollar question: How can an unknown author possibly compete with the 400,000 titles published each year, the million-plus e-books, not to mention the millions of books already in print?

That's where Amazon comes in. This supremely powerful retailer is a self-publisher's best friend. It's by far the strongest platform online with the widest visibility. And, with the recent addition of Kindle Direct Publishing (KDP), it is one of the few places an author can generate helpful publicity for FREE. KDP is a great avenue to help authors gain name recognition, boost book sales and in some cases, land a title in the top 100 bestsellers.

For instance, author Jessica Park eloquently details how Amazon "saved her book" in a blog she posted June 15, 2012 at IndieReader, which was also carried by HuffPost. That same month, Amazon actively promoted Park's blog by posting a letter to its authors on its .com site.

Park is a known commodity, having previously authored five books that had been published through traditional channels. For some strange reason, she had to prove herself again and again with each new work. She only turned to self-publishing in desperation after her latest manuscript, *Flat-Out Love*, was rejected by 14 editors.

It should be noted that *Flat-Out Love* is currently an Amazon bestseller in the Young Adult category!

Connecting to readers, maintaining artistic control of the finished product and holding on to a larger share of revenue were other reasons Park decided to try going "INDIE." She credits KDP and Amazon for her success.

Read Park's full post at: http://indiereader.com/2012/06/how-amazon-saved-my-life/.

How about you? Tired of form rejection letters, unscrupulous publishers or being told you need to totally revise what you've written to make it more "commercial"?
Or maybe you're like Jessica Park; you did get the break you were hoping for … but the publishers insisted you change your content, title and/or book cover before publishing your work. Then, unless you were already a noted author, the publishing house elected to move on to the next client after a few book signings and some early publicity. No wonder that advance you received is evaporating steadily as you buy back your unsold copies.

Maybe it's time to take charge of your creativity and your writing future!

Enjoy and please let us know about your success: @penabook or www.luckycinda.com.

PART I - THE BASICS

Chapter 2 – Writing your book

Selling books in the computer-dominated age demands more than a completed manuscript with a catchy title. You have to create a book you can persuade people to want and you do that by researching consumer needs and habits.

As an example, millions of writers, businesses and non-profit groups are looking to take advantage of the Internet to gain exposure. So people writing books about all avenues of e-promoting, book selling, online marketing or other 21st century advertising methods are bestsellers in this niche.

Specialty topics also sell. Popular cable cooking shows have enhanced the desirability of food-centric how-to books discussing everything from creating fancy French repasts to wrestling a stew from edible odds and ends you might find in a forest. The health sector has also enjoyed flourishing sales for books replete with low-calorie and/or sugarless recipes accompanied by gorgeous photos of finished products.

Identify and investigate your niche by checking out what's hot at online book retailers or at your local book store … or what topics continuously make the bestseller lists. Keep a desktop folder of your findings – the info will come in handy later on.

This exercise will also teach you to look at your finished product with new eyes. Although you wrote for love and not to fit neatly into some hot category, you'll find that your work does have certain criteria in common with other popular books in its classifications – specifics you can use in your advertising.

As a rule, fiction is tougher to sell than non-fiction but for a superb storyteller, this genre can still be lucrative. Informational books need researched, cited and verifiable figures and facts. On the other hand, while research is still essential for a well composed work of fiction, it can become a successful commercial product if fleshed out with unforgettable characters, dialogue that reveals, vivid descriptions and surprising, yet, believable plots.

If you know who your audience is BEFORE you complete your book, you'll know which demographics to target when you're ready to sell. You can create the book for the audience or vice-versa!

Suggestion Numero Uno: Make your product as unique as you. Most people bore easily and avid readers are always seeking the exotic or unfamiliar. Look at the success of *The Hunger Games* series or the erotic *Fifty Shades* trilogy.

Readers embraced these books because of their singular emotional settings, intriguing characters and riveting prose.

Freedom of structure, when adopted correctly, is another self-publishing plus. You don't have to abide to the letter of grammar rules or formats. Finding new ways to tell a story can help you build a reputation as an innovator. Just be sure not to compromise quality. Breaking rules is fine when and if you know what the rules are and can justify breaking them.

Your best possible product is the only one you should ever offer for public consumption.

Most importantly, make your book look and feel like it was published traditionally. Give readers a well-edited, error-free copy, a relevant cover design and a fair price. And be sure to format the piece properly for each new incarnation so that it's attractive and reader friendly.

Section I: The Product – Quality sells

a. Professional Editing:
When people shop for books they look for subjects that appeal, satisfy a need or are written by authors they know. If you want to lure buyers and keep them satisfied, make sure their experience with your manuscript is a pure one.

Uncle Henry's life story might be amazing and inspiring. Your recounting of it might be insightful and tender. But if your book doesn't display error-free copy with professional quality editing, copy editing, design and formatting, you will never capture or retain the interest of a real book lover. Accidental grammar errors, misplaced punctuation, and unintentionally misspelled words will all bounce a reader right out of the text, no matter how poetic or life-altering. The money you spend on professional help – an editor, a copy editor and a proof reader – is the soundest investment you can make in your product.

Expect to pay between $5 and $8 per 1,000 words for these services. Bestselling author, Jeff Bennington, author of *The Indie Author's Guide*, uses Neal Hock from Hock's Editing Services. We work with Elizabeth McAdams of Beaumont Hardy Editing and highly recommend her.

To ensure pristine text, there are plenty of wallet-friendly tools and professionals available that were unknown as recently as five years ago. Unfortunately, too many self-published authors don't take advantage of these services. This is why the stigma of shoddily presented INDIE books still colors the prejudices of major book sellers and industry book buyers. Your diligence will help change that.

Online readers who stumble across your novels, or purchase your book, based on recommendations will be turned off with a sub-standard product. This could lead to ego-deflating book reviews or too frequent refunds associated with your title.

In our opinion, losing credibility is actually worse than losing sales. A good reputation in this business is difficult to assemble yet essential for networking and developing new contacts.

With our first book, *Francesca of Lost Nation*, a major California retailer was reluctant to engage us for an author event because we were self-published. After several conversations with their corporate office and local management, they revealed why: They had been embarrassed by the poor quality of too many self-published books. Customer complaints and book refunds resulted – largely due to too many misspelled words, disjointed plot turns and clunky or dumb sounding dialogue.

Happily, once they read and reviewed *Francesca of Lost Nation* – and were assured it lived up to their standards – they invited us to conduct an event at one of their stores where the book is still available for their customers.

Shameless Plug: *Francesca of Lost Nation* continues to do well. In fact, in June of 2012, it landed in the top 100 paid Kindle books under the categories of History Fiction and Family Relationships. In July, after a KDP promo, Francesca of Lost Nation made the top 100 paid Kindle books for family saga. It continues to do well and even when it dips back into the top 100,000, we are making more monthly sales than before we ever joined KDP-Select. If we can do it, YOU can do it.

b. Title - What's in a name? Everything!
As we mentioned earlier, the book selling process is evolving rapidly. These days, you have to pen a book that you can educate people to buy. Choosing title and chapter headings that incorporate the same phrases your target readers are searching online will make it easier for them to spot your product. You can also use subtitles to let people know in a few words what the book has to offer or what the story is about.

A personal aside: One reason our book, *Francesca of Lost Nation,* didn't get as much initial attention as we hoped was because the title didn't adequately express what the book is about. But when we added a simple subtitle, *"a true novel"* as well as a brief cover description revealing that it's a post WWII adventure romance, sales began to spike.

We learned from our mistakes but it cost us some time and money. If you incorporate an aptly descriptive title, you will avoid our pitfalls and ensure better sales from the get-go.

Other tips for choosing a compelling title:

- Most Internet-savvy people scan for items they want, reading material included. Since it's a physical impossibility to read everything collected by a search engine on a given topic, online-users base their choices on "key words" found in headlines or book descriptions.

- Keep your title as short as possible and to the point. A great example is Dan Brown's monster selling *The DaVinci Code.*

- One-line phrases work beautifully. What is your book really about? Synthesize your answer into a tight group of words that would grab your attention, make you curious and entice you to investigate further: *The Purpose Driven Life* by Rick Warren or *He's Just Not That Into You* by Greg Behrendt and Liz Tuccillo.

Non-fiction titles should reveal what type of information you are offering: *How I Sold a Million Ebooks in Five Months,* by John Locke or *Make A Killing On Kindle (Without Blogging, Facebook; Twitter: The Guerilla Marketer's Guide To Selling Ebooks On Amazon by* Michael Alvear or *$ell More Book$: How to increase sales and Amazon rankings using Kindle Direct Publishing* by Lucinda Sue Crosby and Laura Dobbins

The back cover information or "copy" should include details about your plot, one or two endorsements/reviews, contact information and an attractive picture of you along with three or four sentences about your background. Sales reps, wholesalers and distribution outlets base buying decisions on cover designs and back cover sales copy.

Ebook sales are often driven by impinging blurb descriptions. Amazon recognizes this fact and allows you to change your book description under your KDP account as often as you wish. This is convenient because it allows you to experiment with the wording and gauge the response, all at no cost to you.

For a book cover worksheet, go to book marketing guru and bestselling author Dan Poynter's website: http://parapub.com/sites/para/resources/allproducts.cfm The instant download is FREE.

c. Design – Looking GOOD!

First impressions matter. It's true for people and it's true for books. When competing with thousands of authors releasing titles in your genre, you need one or more components that will make your work stand out in the crowd. When readers are scanning through a list in their topic range, they often decide which books to read based simply on how the book looks. We can't emphasize this enough!

Keep in mind that electronic sales don't usually provide customers an opportunity to physically scan through your pages or examine front and back cover designs. E-purchases will often be based on the response evoked by your thumbnail image. Are your titles, fonts and cover art consistent? Do they suggest the proper mood for your piece? Are they a part of the whole picture/story? Or do they detract or distract?

Section II: Invoke an emotional response – eye-grabbing ideas

a. Believe it or not, less IS more.
Keep it clean and leave plenty of "white space" (empty area). Try to avoid fancy artwork and complicated designs and make sure your fonts can be easily read!

What type of covers pique your interest? Look at books in your genre – and in your personal library – to see what styles or layouts appeal to you most.

b. Mood Indigo - Setting the stage:
The colors and images you use should evoke feelings/impressions in potential buyers. Determine what type of reaction you are seeking and do some research on how to produce that reaction visually.

USA Today took some jabs from design dilettantes and journalism traditionalists on the launch of its newspaper in 1982. Today the Gannet-owned publication is one of the most widely circulated newspapers in the United States, boasting a 1.8 million readership as of March 2012.

USA Today divides its newspaper sections by colors. It uses an easy to read set-up, dozens of images per edition as well as graphics and maps throughout the publication.

Many newspapers across the country carry the same news ... some even employ the same photos and maps. But few have enticed readers the way *USA Today* has done with its innovative presentation.

c. Is a picture worth 1,000 words? Artwork is crucial.
Your cover is the potential buyer's first introduction to your labor of love and its content.

- Bottom line: Don't use an image that distorts the first impression of your story or one that doesn't set the tone properly for what's inside. If possible, pay for a professional to do the work. It costs $349 for a custom cover at Amazon's Createspace.com.

- The Small Publishers, Artists and Writers Network (SPAWN) offer a $100 book design discount to its members for services at: http://www.logicalexpressions.com/

There are reasonably priced and knowledgeable freelance artists. Most professionals host or have access to a web site that carries examples of covers they've created. You'll have to do some nosing around and you might ask around at on-line author forums.

- John Kremer, book marketing expert and bestselling author, has an extensive list of artists at his website: http://www.bookmarket.com/101des.htm.

But if you need to or wish to design the covers yourself, look for royalty-free art or pay someone up front for their photos or graphics. It's less complicated to buy these components outright so you don't have to deal with copyright or use issues later on.

- Dan Poynter, author of *Writing Your Book*, recommends http://www.flickr.com/creativecommons/org and www.clipart.com when building your own covers.

- We've also used www.dreamstime.com and Getty Photos.

d. You need a backbone! Don't forget the spine.

For those of you that desire both digital and print copies, it's important to remember that when standing upright on a shelf, the spine may be all that's visible to a potential reader. This makes it valuable space. The spine should display your name and book title.

e. Where to publish?

Make no mistake: when it comes to controlling the self-publishing process, Amazon is the Champ. We have embraced Createspace and KDP - Select (Kindle Direct Publishing). This allows us to publish our books digitally and physically, whenever we like, in the appropriate quantity.

We recommend Createspace to publish your books and KDP to place them on Kindle.

If you are looking to publish on US Amazon and to the e-stores on Createspace only, it's FREE. However, if you want access to wider distribution, including say, European markets, Createspace's fee is $25 per title.

Amazon additionally offers KDP Select, which allows your book to be borrowed by Amazon "Prime Members." For each book that is borrowed, authors receive a percentage of a KDP Select Fund of $6 million throughout 2012. For example, KDP Select-Enrolled authors earned $2.26 per borrow in May 2012.

Note: If you self published outside of Createspace you can still use Amazon's KDP for free …

1. if you own the rights to your book and
2. it isn't electronically published, or distributed, in its entirety anywhere else, including your website.

Some reformatting will be necessary when converting your manuscripts for Kindle and we will outline those steps later. In addition, Createspace provides a step-by-step cover design tool, directions on how to format and upload your manuscripts and an online proofreader that will enable viewing of your final product before publishing.

If you choose to forgo KDP altogether, or decide to branch out, from exclusively going with Amazon, use Smashwords. They offer top royalties and can distribute your book both in print and digitally. Sign-up is FREE.

Another top print-on-demand service is Lightning Source. This company is a a world-wide wholesaling subsidiary of Ingram Group Content. As of June 2012, Lightning Source charges $75 per title and places your books on Amazon and Barnes and Noble, as well as Baker and Taylor.

Lightning Source is a wholesaler used by most bookstores.

Important Note: If you are using KDP you will not be able to offer your title digitally through Lightning Source during the 90-day exclusivity that Amazon requires. We should also point out that Createspace also uses Lightning Source to make your books available at book stores. You'll have to contact each company or read their guidelines to see what works best for your needs.

In addition, there are several other printers and Indie companies that can also give you large printing and distribution. We prefer Amazon because of its name recognition, its openness to self-publishers and the success it has offered us. But you should pursue your own desires and research what works best for you.

f. Format to E-books
Explaining all the technical intricacies of formatting documents for digital publishing would be like trying to solve trigonometry problems without having taken any math classes. If you're not A. Einstein, we'll outline the ABCs and a listing of free reference guides that explain formatting step-by-step. Amazon, by the way, offers free how-to information online.

Like any other aspect of writing and publishing books, proper formatting is a must. If your copy has spacing problems, or if the information is laid out confusingly, you will frustrate your reader and lose sales Make sure chapter headings are placed uniformly on the page.

Beware of unaccountable errors, or strange symbols, as you go along. Amazon will convert your files but sometimes special characters or headings don't look as you had planned. It's important to review your copies carefully. We actually suggest converting to e-book format PRIOR to uploading to KDP.

Important Note: Photos can be misplaced during the conversion for no apparent reason!!!!! Logically, more images equal more formatting challenges. Personal tribulations include our latest release, *The Adventures of Baylard Bear: a story about being DIFFERENT.* Because it's a children's book, we decided we'd format for large print. In addition, the book needed to measure 8 X 11 to better showcase the images. However, converting our product to an ebook required us to reduce both the text and image sizes. You'll have to invest some time and energy to discover what works best for your manuscript. OR outsource it to a professional.

The easiest method is to create the original text-only document in Microsoft Word and then convert it using free conversion software. Please check out the following sites:

http://ebook.online-convert.com/convert-to-epub

http://www.epubconverter.org/

In conclusion:
It took us quite a lot of trial and error (emphasize on ERROR) when we began converting our books. But even as you read this, the process for Do-It-Yourself (DIY) authors to make their e-books available globally is becoming less convoluted. We advise patience, perseverance and 17 pots of chamomile tea.

If you don't want to hassle with formats, it should cost between $100 and $200 to hire a pro to do it for you.

The Conversion Process in a nutshell:

1. Write a text-only document in Microsoft Word
2. Set your margin sizes (we prefer .5)
3. Set your indent with automatic formatting
4. Use images prudently

5. Keep it simple – formatting headlines, subheads, chapters and other elements for digital devices is different than for a print version
6. SAVE OFTEN!!!

Recommended FREE books to help you:

1. *Building Your Book for Kindle* by Amazon KDP
http://www.amazon.com/dp/B007URVZJ6/

2. *Building Your Book for Kindle for MAC* by Amazon KDP
http://www.amazon.com/dp/B00822K3Z0/

3. *Smashwords Style Guide – How to Format Your Ebook* (Smashwords Guide) by Mark Coker
http://www.amazon.com/dp/B004XWJ7UK/

g. Pricing – Be honest … How much would YOU pay?
Digital books are expected to cost less than hard copies. An average for new authors runs between 99 cents and $2.99 per download. Amazon encourages writers to price their work between $2.99 and $9.99 by offering a 70 percent author profit. The lower end titles, $2.99 and less, only earn a 35 percent author share, but in some cases sell at a larger volume.

If you become a bestseller, or offer a rare yet highly sought-after topic with little competition, you can set a higher price and take the 35 percent profit Amazon offers for titles $9.99 or more. This process is not a science, it's an art. Experimentation is the only way to find out what works best for a particular work.

Amazon allows tremendous flexibility in both Createspace and KDP … and they don't cost you a dime! Read through the criteria at both Createspace and KDP. Distribution costs may alter minimum price points for print copies.

Section III: Setting up for sales

Before venturing into the big wide world with your latest novel, memoir, or how-to, you should draw up or jot down a marketing plan. You'll need to establish a REALITY-BASED budget, a time table and a to-do list. We recommend developing this fluid document on your computer and putting a shortened version on a dry erase board. Hang this board in a prominent place where you'll see it every blasted day.

Early on, you should decide if you want a website, a blog, or both. We recommend both if at all feasible because web sites and blogs are a modern writer's tools when building and sustaining credibility, a fan base and a writing persona or brand. They also provide a place for the continuous shameless promotion you will need, an easily located forum for selling your products and a central way for you to be contacted.

a. Website - getting the word OUT

- Basic Information – a one-stop shop where readers learn about you and your work

- Promotion – placing contact information on your marketing packets, your book covers and letter heads gives you credibility

- Interaction – your site gives you a platform to communicate with your readers and potential buyers

First off, you'll need a domain name and a place to host your site. Make your domain name short, easy to remember and one that identifies your brand. And purchase dot.com domains instead of .net or .org.

Secondly, choose a webhost. We use Hostgator. You can evaluate the top ten webhosts, their costs and browse product and service ratings/reviews at: http://www.webhostingchoice.com.

What should you include on your site?
At minimum, post a picture of yourself with a short bio and contact information. Include an image of your book cover, a short summary of your book, the purchase price and other pertinent information. You should link to your Amazon site and/or to a purchase page like PayPal.

How much information you want to include on your website and how often you want to update the content is up to you. Statistics show that authors who regularly refresh images and/or information, and those who stay connected with their readers, build a higher online visibility and sell more books.

A publisher polling firm, *The Codex Group*, recently released a 2011 study:

- showing that author websites are one of the key factors in book purchasing decisions

- demonstrating that websites are the preferred method for consumers' interaction with their favorite authors

- indicating that "book shoppers who visited authors' websites bought 38 percent more books, from a wider range of retailers, than those who had not visited an author site"

To learn more about this study:
http://www.thebookdoctors.com/does-an-author-really-need-a-website-the-book-doctors-interview-annik-lafarge-on-how-to-be-a-more-effective-author-online

Other author web site benefits:

- a place to capture emails to build lists for future sales

- a platform for distributing newsletters, personal appearance schedules or announce awards

- a way to capitalize on additional revenue opportunities through affiliate programs or paid advertising

- a forum to express yourself freely

Why have a website AND a blog? What's the difference?
Think of your website as a storefront on "Book Street." It has an address where you can be located and communicated with. It displays "you" and your products. It doesn't often require a new coat of paint or customized awning but it does allow shoppers who've made up their minds to navigate to your purchase page.

For authors who don't want to spend a lot of time updating information or working online, we recommend getting a website and referring to it like you would your Amazon page on:

- Social Media Accounts

- Blog posts

- Online Advertisements

- In your promotional packets

Why a blog?
A blog is a form of advertising with world-wide distribution outlets at no cost. You can talk to people on forums, social groups and through email lists. Succinctly, it's global access at your fingertips.

Blogs are incredibly useful for engaging newcomers, creating a buzz about new information and revitalizing old information. If you're unfamiliar with the lingo, think of them as electronic magazines or flexible and fluid marketing tools … unlike the "fixed" aspect of your store front. If people like what you have to offer, they will share it with others on their social media sites – FREE publicity!

In addition, if you are an Amazon associate, you can list Amazon products on your site for sale and make a small commission every time someone makes a purchase through your blog.

1. Be creative: "Clever" will bring people back.
There's a bookseller on Facebook who encourages writers to post a phrase or sentence from page 99 of their book. If people are intrigued enough with the author's line, they will often click on his or her book to see what comes next.

Here are some examples from the site: (http://page99.in/blog/):

- "Whenever I see a weirdly shaped garbage bag, … I always wonder if it's the one with a dead body in it." (*PostSecret: Confessions on Life, Death and God* by Frank Warren)

- "If You Stare Long Enough at Serious People They will Begin to Appear Comical." (*Serious Men* by Manu Joseph)

2. How a blog helps you earn credibility and build visibility:
As you learn more about online marketing, you will realize the importance of high rankings on search pages. (The topic itself is complex and an entirely different book – coming soon!)

When writing blog posts, you should try to include keywords that people are using to search online. For instance, if you wrote a how-to book about marketing, your articles/blurbs should reference "book marketing" or "how to market a book" as well as other key phrases ... ones that you should also have included in your book title, subtitle, book content and book thumbnails.
If your book is a Romance Novel, some of your keywords might be "romance fiction" "love mystery" or "books about romance." Depending on the type of romance, you could employ more specific phrases like "historic romance novel" or "family saga friendship."

Picture yourself looking for a book similar to the one you wrote and select words you would type into the search engines. As easily as that, you have identified your first set of marketing phrases.

3. A blog takes time not money
Keeping your blog fresh, will require TIME and there is some skill involved in developing your brand using keywords on services like Twitter and Facebook. But if you can write something interesting, catchy or thought provoking at least twice a week, you will drive traffic to your product pages.

Important Note: If you have a full-time job, this may not be your best route. You'll probably need to hire someone or add paid advertising to your budget.

b. An Honest Budget – More Planning; Less Spending
Price is one of the big plus points of digital publishing. However, unless you are already a hideously famous writer, you could go broke trying to get your book noticed. Even experienced writers often fail to prepare for the unexpected, yet unavoidable financial

outlays of self-publishing. Aside from paying professional editors and book designers, there are a number of other expenses to consider.

1. Copyrights and identification numbers
Bookstores require an International Standard Book Number (ISBN). This will identify your work's publisher and allow you to sell books to retailers, libraries and bookstores. An ISBN costs $125 each or come in bundles of 10 for $240.
Obtaining a Library of Congress number is free but you will have to pay postage to send your finished product and it will cost $45 to secure the actual copyright. Although some printing companies will obtain these numbers for you, you'll still be responsible for processing fees.

In the digital world, these expenses are greatly reduced.

GO AMAZON: Createspace offers authors four ISBN options including a FREE Createspace-Assigned ISBN.
Whether you choose Print on Demand or use a traditional printer for your hard copies, set money aside for "production costs" – like printing and shipping which run anywhere from $2.50 to $20 per title. The amount is determined by the size of your book, page count, images and whether or not you use color.

If you use KDP exclusively, your books will only be available electronically, so no printing costs are deducted from your royalties.

How much you make with your electronic files on KDP depends on how much your book costs to buy. If you price it between $2.99 and $9.99, you will earn 70 percent royalty for each e-copy sold.

Createspace allows you to offer a paper copy of your book, which is only printed after an order is placed. Createspace deducts the cost of printing and takes a percentage of the sale, leaving you to collect whatever is left. For a $15 book, the writer's share would be around $5.

Now let's consider other – more hidden – costs.

2. Advertising – getting the word out isn't cheap

For Print Copies:
After you've exhausted all the obvious initial promotional opportunities – like selling to friends and family; hitting the local newspaper and radio stations; and conducting signings for nearby libraries, book stores or book clubs – you will need to pay for advertising.

Marketing accessories for print or digital books:
The following might or might not be deemed necessary but should definitely be considered. Remember, you are creating a business!

- Business cards

- Stationary

- Postage to send out review requests

- Book giveaways

- Flyers

- Brochures

- Press Kits

- Online advertising

Tip: Be wary of buying into programs that charge for building social media pages and promise overnight success. And watch out for "publicity hounds" that guarantee television spots.

There are reputable services but there are also hundreds if not thousands of companies preying on new authors. Instead of paying someone $5,000 to promote you, invest in some reasonably priced online ads or buy coupons to help people purchase your book.

c. Time management – Make yourself accountable!
If you are operating within a strict and/or limited budget and can't afford hired help, you'll absolutely positively need a written schedule. We recommend making a list and setting aside 8 to 16 hours each week to complete your tasks.

- Sending out press releases

- Blogging

- Setting up online ads

- Making time for interviews, book signings, public or online appearances

- Keeping abreast of orders, emails or phone calls

- Setting up appointments, speaking engagements, signings

- Posting to social media – especially during a KDP promotion

d. Establish a Marketing Plan

Money and time will determine the complexity and duration of your marketing plan.

1. When selling hard copies:
Determine the best way to reach your intended audience and plan accordingly. There are a number of options you can mix and match for the most comprehensive and affordable outreach program.

- Ads in newspapers or magazines – this can be expensive and inefficient for unknown authors.

- Compare the cost of advertising in your local Swap Sheet, Penny Saver or other weekly ad-based giveaway.

- Book signings inviting friends and relatives, as well as their friends and relatives, can be cost effective if the venue advertises your appearance. Be sure to factor in mileage, meals and lodging fees, if appropriate.

- Book fairs and festivals all entail vendor costs, table fees, travel and lodging.

- Online advertising

- Direct mail or email advertising

2. KDP – Digital sales only

- Plan FREE promotions well in advance and consider holiday gift-giving patterns.

- Purchase paid ads before and after your free promotions.

- Experiment with lower-than-usual price manipulation to get your book bought after the free promotions.

- Since ongoing advertising will be necessary, determine how much you want to pay per month or annually.

- Provide free copies for ebook reviewers

Note: Author Joanna Penn offers a copy of her Award-winning marketing plan as a free download on her website: http://www.thecreativepenn.com/2009/02/20/award-winning-marketing-plan/

Part II - The Essentials

Chapter 3 – Credibility: Awards and Reviews and How to Generate Them

Winning contests and great book reviews doesn't guarantee sales but it doesn't hurt either. Quality, however, still counts more than quantity. If you have too many awards – especially from unknown organizations – or too many reviews with unknown reviewers, it turns off readers.

Go after two or three good reviews and submit your book to legitimate book contests.

Contests:
Awards give your books credibility and let people know others have recognized the value of your product. INDIE authors who partake in contests open to self-publishers also get free marketing tips – a great bonus. Don't pay more than $100 to enter unless it's a recognized company with a reputable history – like an Amazon or Writers Digest.

We recommend the following:
California Book Contest – http://bookcontest.luckycinda.com/
(This is a competition we sponsor and will be seeking entries in Septemeber 2012)

Dan Poynter's Global Ebook Awards -
http://globalebookawards.com/
(We were judges and participants in 2012)

Amazon Novel Award - https://www.createspace.com/abna

Writer's Digest Self-Published Book Awards –
http://www.writersdigest.com/competitions/selfpublished

See John Kremer's extensive list of book contests at:
http://www.bookmarket.com/awards.htm

Book Reviews: We cannot stress the following sentence enough: GOOD AND TRUSTED REVIEWS ARE ESSENTIAL FOR BOOK SALES.

Unfortunately, INDIE authors rarely have access to traditional reviewers, so landing a rave write-up in *The Los Angeles Times* or the *New York Times* isn't a reality-based option. Big-name book reviewers are loyal to traditional publishing concerns and have shut out folks like us.

The good news is that there are many online readers willing to give book reviews as well as an ever increasing number of reputable book forums seeking books to review.

Amazon is a good place to start.

As you browse through books in your genre, you will see a list of book reviews for each title. If you click on the name of a reviewer, you should discover a personal profile that often lists an email address. In some cases the person will mention books or categories of books they are interested in reviewing.

Amazon also compiles its own list of book reviewers. By scanning their information, you can find out what type of books they like to read and whether or not they are accepting submissions. http://www.amazon.com/review/top-reviewers.

Book-centric websites and forums are a great place to find people who are looking for books to review.

Meet the Author Forums – is an e-community on Amazon where authors can plug their books. Follow the threads **-a grouping of posts set-up as a conversation among users -** there are readers who will announce they are seeking books to review. (Amazon.com – sign in and click on discussions)

- GoodReads – is one of the largest and most active e-sites for author/reader discussions. You'll come across an array of on-going forums and groups seeking books to read, review and even share. GoodReads is extremely author-friendly. (http://www.goodreads.com/)

- The Midwest Book Review site welcomes self-publishers. Aside from offering a long-list of helpful information, the blog also includes an extensive list of other Book Review sites.
  (http://www.midwestbookreview.com/index.html)

- The Book Blogger Directory provides a comprehensive list of book bloggers that review books.
  (http://bookbloggerdirectory.wordpress.com/)

Other sites worth exploring:

Step by Step Self-Publishing Blog
http://www.stepbystepselfpublishing.net/reviewer-list.html

Book Marketing and Book Promotion
http://www.bookmarket.com/magazines-books.htm

Important Note: We advise against paid reviews. There are more than enough people within easy online access who are reading books and posting quality reviews at no cost.

Chapter 4 – Social Media – Is it really necessary?

Unless you have money to hire online marketing pros, you will need to delve into the world of social media. At the minimum, you should become familiar with the ins and outs of Twitter and Facebook. When you are ready to launch your KDP promotions, these are the perfect forums to help you advertise your books – and in most cases, this activity is FREE.

Twitter and Facebook are loaded with promotional tools. Just follow their guidelines and use these opportunities wisely. Communicating on Twitter and Facebook is a fluid exercise like your blog. You'll want to offer a flow of information, refresh the buzz on old and new products and engage in conversations.

Both sites offer search technologies that specialize in locating target audiences. For example, if you are seeking fiction readers and reviewers, you would search for "book clubs" "fiction groups" and "book reviewers."

Get acquainted with these sites. As your writing career evolves, these forums will become more useful.

Twitter Tips:
Some people on Twitter seek book recommendations. Here's how to find them – In the search box, type "book recommendations," "kindle suggestions," "fiction readers," or "book clubs."

Twitter allows you to message these people directly by using their twitter signatures. For example, if you were to send us a message, it would look like this: @penabook Here is a book suggestion for you: Francesca of Lost Nation, **http://tinyurl.com/d3daktm**.

This message is public so be professional and helpful. Don't only plug your book. If you want to send a private direct message, the person needs to be one of your followers. Usually if you follow someone they will follow you back.

You can also use Twitter for research. For instance, if you are seeking accounts that tweet about Kindle books, you can type Kindle Books in the search box or use hashtags #kindlebooks to find people to message or follow.

Another research advantage is to find people whose expertise or services may help you. For example, our book, *"The Adventures of Baylard Bear – a story about being DIFFERENT,"* has an adoption theme so we could do a search on the word "adoption" to find people interested in the subject. Or we could find possible organization to contact that could be interested in buying our book for their groups.

Facebook Tips: Using this social site is similar to Twitter but you can't promote directly like you can on Twitter. For example, you can't contact people on Facebook unless they are friends with you. If you try to connect with too many people that don't know you, Facebook will boot you off their system.

What you can do is this: Join conversations about books, authors or literature available in digital form. If someone asks you directly about something, including your books or services, you can respond.

If you have books to market for KDP promotion days, there are some sites on Facebook that allow you to post your FREEBIES. Read each site's guidelines.

In general, while tweeting a 100 times a day is common, posting to Facebook – for promotional purposes – should be limited to no more than 2 or 3 times a day.

Recommended Books:

How To Facebook - The No Nonsense Guide To Using Facebook by Dave Barry (on Kindle at Amazon)

The Insider's Guide To Becoming a Twitter Marketing Pro by Craig Kelley (on Kindle at Amazon)

Chapter 5 – Setting Up KDP

Amazon provides a step-by-step guide on how to set up your manuscripts on Kindle Direct Publishing. We are also including some little-known recommendations crucial for good rankings.

1. Choosing the most effective keywords
Amazon allows you seven key words or keyword phrases when uploading your manuscript to KDP. Pick the words that best describe your book CAREFULLY.

Again, select descriptive phrases or sets of words appropriate for an Amazon search. For example, if you are seeking a new romance novel, you would type the phrase "new romance novel," into the search box. If you have that same phrase in your key word selections, your book would be included on the list of new romance novels.

But hey! You'll be up against tens of thousands of other new romance novels! It will be a dog's age-and-a-half before anyone arrives at your title, that's why working Amazon book categories is so vital to your ultimate success.

2. Categories:

Amazon allows you to place your title under two categories at a time and it is this placement that determines your competition.

Our test case: As we write this, our novel *Francesca of Lost Nation* is in the same categories as Kristin Hannah's *Firefly Lane*:

Books -Literature & Fiction -Women's Fiction - Friendship
Kindle Store -Kindle eBooks – Fiction - Genre Fiction -Family Saga

It's impossible to compete with a bestselling author like Hannah, not to mention all the other famous folks in the Fiction Categories. But the subcategories of Family Saga and Friendship, also appropriately descriptive for our purposes, are good alternates.

Digital Book Today site owner, Anthony Wessel, is in the business of helping authors and decided he needed to learn the process of

Kindle publishing to better inform his audience.

Wessel wrote a short story about taking his 85-year-old dad to Washington D.C. and experimented with the categories. Using an informal category exercise, (listed below), his book is now a "bestseller" – in the Top 100 – in three categories.

There is no reason you can't do the same.

However, for some reason, Amazon doesn't make it easy to place your book in the proper subcategories, so again, you'll have to experiment. If all else fails, contact Amazon and ask them which category would be best for your book.

NOTE: Author Hope Welsh posted an incredibly helpful article on how to place your book in the proper categories. Find here: http://digitalbooktoday.com/getting-your-ebook-in-the-proper-category-for-improved-ranking/

3. Write a spot-on description
The description of your book should contain phrases from your keyword and category selections without making it sound silly or overly commercial.

Remember, your description should be enticing enough to make the reader want to buy your book. Be conscientious about intentionally misleading! You could wind up stuck with refunds AND Amazon could even remove your title!

4. Author Page
Amazon allows you to post an Author's Page which is similar to a blog. You can include detailed information about yourself and post pictures and videos along with links to your website and blogs. This is a great opportunity for you to connect with your readers.
You're ready to start promoting.

Part III - Action plan

Chapter 6 – Getting your book into reader's hands

How well are you selling? That's the first question you need to ask yourself before deciding whether KDP Select is your solution to getting your book noticed. If you're reading this book, chances are you're a great fit.

Like any selling concept, there are pros and cons built into KDP Select. For the author who isn't selling like hotcakes, this program will weigh heavily on the pro side!!!

KDP Select Pros

a. This program welcomes INDIE authors and titles

b. It jumpstarts your Amazon rankings

c. You can generate an amazing amount of FREE publicity

d. You have a real chance to land in the top 100 for your category – a tremendous selling point

e. You can create increased book sales

f. You have the possibility of becoming a top paid bestseller

KDP Select Cons

a. If you are already making steady sales and your book rankings are acceptable to you, you may not wish to grant KDP Select exclusivity.

b. Before working KDP Select, you'll need to take down your digital book displays from your own website, Smashwords, Barnes and Noble and anywhere else you were distributing electronic copies – including your own sites.

As INDIE authors, we use KDP Select because we believe it is the most powerful tool for the self-published. We have experienced the real benefits of the program and highly recommend it. But you need to decide for yourself if it's the right path for your product, your attitude and your perseverance level. So evaluate carefully.

Here's how KDP Select works:

1. Amazon requires a 90-day exclusive.
2. In exchange, Amazon lists your titles with their Lending Library and Amazon allows their Prime members – who pay an annual fee - to borrow one ebook a month at no charge.

3. In addition, authors are given five FREE promotion days for each 90-day period while enrolled in KDP Select.

Some authors are reluctant to embrace the program because they are required to offer a book at no cost on these five promotion dates. However, if no one ever hears about your book, it will never become a quantity seller, much less a best seller.

Here's how Amazon helped us.

We released *Francesca of Lost Nation* in mid-2010. That first year, we had managed to sell nearly 1,000 copies of our book. But by 2011, our rankings at Amazon for Kindle were hovering near 600,000.

By early 2012, the book had moved up some but still lingered in the 400,000 range. Like Jessica Park, we decided we had nothing to lose by trying the KDP program. We pulled the novel's digital distribution from our other sites and went exclusively with Amazon.

And Amazon KDP made us a bestseller.

Between June 3 and June 4, 2012, *Francesca of Lost Nation* was #1 in three categories: Family Relationships, Friendship and Historic Fiction. In addition, our book made the top 100 list for FREE e-books.

Once we switched our title from FREE to PAID, we remained in the top 100 paid Kindle categories for nine days. Our Kindle sales for that period amounted to about $500 – an amazing result for what was basically an experiment.

Interestingly, the benefits of those efforts are still echoing loud and long. *Francesca of Lost Nation* continues to SELL steadily, with a constant attendant Amazon ranking well above the 400,000 status we once owned. On average, we tend to rank between 28,000 and 54,000. Of course, the rate of sales slows as others promote their books. In any event, we plan to continue with our free and paid promotions until the book hits that top 100 paid list on a continuing basis.

From the outset of this journey, we KNEW we had a tremendous product in *Francesca of Lost Nation* – people absolutely love it. To date, it's won five literary awards and garnered dozens of glowing reviews on sites across the Internet. But how to get it noticed on a broad scale stumped us.

Our main goal with KDP was simply to get our book into reader's hands ... something we accomplished in spades. Between June 3 and June 4, more than 10,000 people downloaded *Francesca of Lost Nation*. The free exposure has also spurred a rash of new blog tours and interviews. But most importantly, it's led to even more reader reviews and steadily increasing revenue.

We have cringed a few times knowing 10,000 copies were downloaded for FREE. Even at .99 each, that would have been a whacking good profit. But we also know that without the FREE promos, our book would have remained near the bottom of Amazon rankings. When it comes to promoting an intellectual property, a person's willingness to take a chance often depends on how much he or she believes in the end product. It took a leap of faith; we jumped and landed in high cotton.

And think how much this far flung publicity would have COST! Without a miracle, convincing 10,000 people to download our book would have been prohibitively expensive.

Besides, it isn't just our digital sales that spiked; our physical inventory is moving too – resulting in even more $$$. AMAZON, we salute you.

Yes … We know it sounds counterintuitive … maybe even crazy. But FREE is the word and KDP Select is the tool. These are the keys to getting your book into thousands of reader's hands who will, in turn, help you get your book into thousands of additional reader's hands. With KDP Select, Amazon has provided one of the most innovative, respected and creative international platforms ever. All you have to do is take advantage.

Chapter 7 – Making Sales and How to Promote

There are several sites that will post your KDP Promotions for FREE. Paid advertisements are certainly one way to go but we believe there are enough reputable FREE options available. We recommend saving your money for the inevitable moment when your rankings succumb to gravity and start to sag.

Before you begin any marketing adventure, be sure your book is ready for success. Do you have that great cover we mentioned earlier? How about thoughtful and emotional content? Did you format your book properly and is the copy clean as a whistle? How many 4 or 5-star ratings and reviews do you have? Are the description blurbs catchy? (Yes, plural; you'll need more than one.) Have you nailed down your key words and phrases?

Then let's get to it!

a. Pick the title, or titles, you want to promote. It's much easier to run one book promotion at a time but if you're a talented high-speed "juggler," go for it.

b. Determine how many days you will use of the five available. Statistics show that running your FREE promotions for 2 days works best. Then wait six weeks and do it again for 2 days.

c. Select the dates carefully with an eye on upcoming noted "buying holidays," like Christmas and Valentine's Day. Friday through Sunday appear to be Prime for purchasing while Monday and Tuesday produce fewer sales. You should consider offering free promotions on a particular day each month.

d. Promote your KDP Select Free Days
The more sites and forums that hear about your book, the more successful your campaign will be. It isn't enough to post an announcement on your blog or to send out a couple of tweets. Get the news out to every person you know on every social site you frequent.

It takes thousands of downloads to move your book up the Amazon rankings. If you don't use your FREE promos properly, you will miss out on a "golden" opportunity.

e. Follow the Free Promotions with layered advertising
For example, the day before your promotions you might buy an ad from World Literary Café called "Social Media Book Buzz" – where your book is promoted on their site and tweeted across several of their Triberr accounts.

Then a day or two after your FREE promotions, you might have purchased an ad from The Kindle Book Review where your book's strategic placement will gain it broader exposure.

Digital Book Today is very author friendly and offers both paid and free promotions. Take advantage and schedule to coordinate dates with your FREE promos.

In this fashion, you can spread out your advertising and time all your marketing campaign components to wring the most out of your investment. The idea is to get as much notice for your book as possible and convert that into sales.

WHERE to PROMOTE:

Important Note: We suggest you have a separate email account attached to your KDP promos. Many of the sites listed below require you to register for newsletters or notifications and your email box will overflow!

You can always opt-out of any subscriptions once you end your promotions. Be sure to read and comply with all site guidelines.

Listings like these can change or disappear without notice. As of press time, the following were still valid:

Kindle Book Promotion Websites
These sites offer free and paid advertising – some require registration and at least a 30 day notice. Most sites need a minimum 3-day notice, so plan ahead.

http://kindlebookpromos.luckycinda.com

http://digitalbooktoday.com/

http://worldliterarycafe.com/

http://thekindlebookreview.blogspot.com/

http://thekindleromancereview.blogspot.com/

http://thewomensnest.com/content/social_media_mania_get_marketing_buzz_your_book

http://ebookswag.com/

http://kindlenationdaily.com/

http://www.centsibleereads.com/

http://www.99-cent-network.com/www.99-cent-Network.com/Home.html

http://www.independentauthornetwork.com/index.html

http://www.kindleboards.com/
http://blog.booksontheknob.org/p/about-this-blog-and-contact-info.html

http://addictedtoebooks.com/submission

http://authormarketingclub.com/members/submit-your-book/

http://bargainebookhunter.com/feature-your-book/

http://ereadernewstoday.com/ent-free-book-submissions/

http://www.freebooksy.com/

http://flurriesofwords.blogspot.com/

http://www.indiebookslist.com/kdp-select-submission-form/

http://www.mediabistro.com/appnewser/category/free-ebooks

http://www.pixelofink.com/sfkb/

http://snickslist.com/books/place-ad/

http://storyfinds.com/

http://www.ereaderiq.com/free/
Fill out the contact form

http://www.fkbooksandtips.com/
Send email to Michael Gallagher – kindle@gagler.com

http://cheapkindledaily.wordpress.com/

http://thefrugalereader.wufoo.com/forms/frugal-freebie-submissions/

Facebook:
Facebook offers a number of sites that allow postings – read each forum's guidelines prior to promoting your book.

- Consider "liking" these sites in exchange for their help

- Posting on Facebook for this type of promotion is best done early on the morning of your campaign's first day or once the day before and once on the day of. Posting too often can be considered "spamming."

http://www.facebook.com/dailynews22
(KindleBookPromos)

http://www.facebook.com/allthingskindle
Site requires a five day advance notice contact – stepartdesigns@hotmail.com

http://www.facebook.com/AontheC
http://www.facebook.com/authormarketingclub

http://www.facebook.com/BookGoodies

http://www.facebook.com/earthsbooknook

http://www.facebook.com/eReader1

http://www.facebook.com/freeebookdeal

http://www.facebook.com/fkbooksandtips

http://www.facebook.com/galleycat/app_4949752878

http://www.facebook.com/iauthor

http://www.facebook.com/IndieBookLounge

http://www.facebook.com/IndieKindleWLC

http://www.facebook.com/kindle

http://www.facebook.com/KindleFreebies

http://www.facebook.com/KindleKorner

http://www.facebook.com/kindledailydeal

http://www.facebook.com/readingkindle

http://www.facebook.com/TheKindleObsessed

http://www.facebook.com/weloveebooks

http://www.facebook.com/StoryFinds

http://www.facebook.com/BookLending

http://www.facebook.com/pages/UK-Kindle-Book-Lovers/175617412524192

http://www.facebook.com/groups/341840249197060

http://www.facebook.com/groups/UK.Kindle.Reading

Twitter – Contact accounts that tweet and retweet (RT) about books

@penabook
@4FreeKindleBook
@BookBub
@DigitalBKToday
@DigitalInkToday
@FreeReadFeed
@KindleFreeBook
@KindleBookKing

@kindleebooks
@TheLuvOfBooks
@Kindlestuff
@KindleEbooksUK
@fkbt
@FreeKindleDude
@FreeKindleBooks
@FreeReadFeed
@PixelofInk
@WLCauthor
@kindlenews

In Twitter's search box also look for book bloggers, ebook readers and book clubs. These Twitters may also be willing to promo your titles. Make sure not to spam them or you will turn off potential readers.

You might also make use of the following sites to help with your Twitter efforts:

http://worldliterarycafe.com/
Has twitter programs including RT teams.

http://www.booktweetingservice.com/
Offers paid RT programs.

Tips: Ask your followers to RT your postings and use hashtags (#), then use words with your hashtags, like #KindleBook #Freebook #Fiction – whatever applies to your title.

Other places you might try:

a. LinkedIn Groups – post at forums you have joined that allow listings of ebooks

b. Yahoo Groups – you will have to join each group before you can post and each has its own rules, so be sure to read the guidelines.

c. Amazon/Kindle Forums
You're restricted to post exclusively at the "Meet Our Authors" section but there are many threads you can use.

Don't forget the foreign boards at Amazon's UK, Denmark, Spain, France and Italy sites. There are thousands of English - speaking readers in those countries.

UK Kindle Users Forum:
http://www.kuforum.co.uk/kindleusersforum/

d. KDP Community Forum
http://forums.kindledirectpublishing.com/kdpforums/forumindex.jsp
a

e. Google + groups
f. Blogs, electronic magazines, newsletters and other sites hosted by people in your field or by readers and reviewers seeking books … You'll have to search for these online, at social media sites and through Twitter.

A good place to start: Listorious – a listing of the top 2 million Twitter Users - http://listorious.com/

Here's the plan, Stan – setting up your KDP Promotion:

1. Select your "for FREE" dates – try a 2-day promotion first. Wait about six weeks and schedule a second promotion for either 2 or 3 days.

2. Announce your promotion in your blog. Ideally you should write a post two to three days prior to your launch and write another post on the day of your promotion.

3. INVEST IN PAID ADVERTISING. Set up your paid ads to run a day or two after your FREE days. If you have the funds, invest in additional ads two weeks after your campaigns. (Many advertising sites sell out early for holiday traffic, so you need to purchase these ads as soon as you can.)

4. Use a service like http://hootsuite.com to schedule hourly tweets for the day of your promotion. You'll want to have at least three different announcements about your book in revolving release during the two-day campaign. Include hash-tagged words like #books,

#Free, #Kindle, #readers, and so forth in your 140 character text for Twitter.

5. If you have a mailing list, Facebook friends or Twitter followers, contact them to see if they would post your promo and in turn ask their friends to post your promo on your launch day.

6. Get ready to post your FREE book announcement on all the sites we've listed or any others you may learn about. Remember some sites require prior notification, so don't wait until the last minute.

ON the DAY of YOUR PROMOTION:

1. Get up early and post your announcement on the Facebook sites, Amazon Author Forums and the Kindle Boards. Also use your Twitter and website accounts to update your readers throughout the day. If you have a mailing list, notify them the day before and the day of your promotion.

2. Promote your blog post through http://pingomatic.com/ and other social forums like Digg and Technorati.

3. Direct message your followers (preferably the ones interested in free books or sharing information about books) the day before and ask if they too will post your freebies on the day of your promotion. You can also tweet them publically with their @name too.

4. Monitor your free downloads and keep track of the information to update your blog and tweets the day after the promotions stop. It's FUN watching your book climb the charts even if you are not getting paid – yet – for sales.

How you promote after your FREE campaign ends will determine your sales. Amazon has provided a super-charged opportunity to generate "book-buzz" for your titles; now it's up to you to capitalize.

Don't get discouraged if the first round doesn't go as well as you imagined. Marketing involves science and art. Analyze what happened and learn from your mistakes. You may need more positive reviews/ratings. You may have to sharpen tweets or other press materials. Once you've made some corrections in your presentation, try, try again.

Chapter 8 – After KDP … S-T-R-E-T-C-H-I-N-G out the "Book Buzz!"

Most authors will see an immediate spike in their book's ranking during KDP Freebies. Some are lucky enough to sustain the wave for a week or two. But at some point, your numbers will hit the skids. Here are some suggestions to help you stay on top longer and maintain sales levels.

DON'T STOP PROMOTING – Relentless is good

1. If you purchased ads (and we hope you did), they should begin running four to five days after your giveaway period.

2. Use Facebook, Twitter, your blog and any other sites you can access to continue chat/discussion about your book. This is the time to blow your horn about the success of your 2-day KDP.

Important Note: Be careful not to oversell or you come across as a spammer. And ALWAYS include a link to your book.
Here are examples of appropriate messages:

"Wow, thanks to all for making me #5 in the friendship category on Kindle during my Free Promos!"

"Francesca of Lost Nation makes top 100 list for #romance history, still available for only $2.99 on #kindle" – http://www.amazon.com/dp/B003MGKA5Y/"

Tip: You can go to http://tinyurl.com to shorten your links if necessary to conform to the 140 character limit requirements of Twitter.

3. Follow-up on comments and emails from people who contact you after reading your book.

4. Continue your regular marketing campaigns. Send out a press release or two about your new rankings – which will have converted to paid Kindle sales. During this period, your rating should remain high.

If you live in small or rural communities, these types of stories are likely to be appealing to your local media, like newspapers and radio stations. Take advantage!

When the FREEBIES end:

Once in a great while, an author will become an instant paid bestseller and ride the rankings for two or three months. But most will start to see a dip in their rankings a week or two after the KDP endeavors, in spite of sales and royalties from the Lending Program. (More on this later)

If you feel your sales were adequate, or better than adequate, for the amount of time, energy and money you invested, schedule another promotion for six weeks out. You can employ many of the materials, strategies and key words/phrases you used the first time around with slight variations.

If your sales were disappointing, it's time to regroup. Consider making some noticeable changes – to your book cover; book descriptions or categories; number or type of reviews; and/or a revision of press releases and tweets to create more drama and interest. Once you've determined why the process didn't produce a satisfactory result, try again.

Important note: Keep your marketing efforts fresh. Fortunately there are a slew of FREE opportunities.

1. Kindle Book Promos – This is one of our sites where we offer free author interviews, title listings and KDP promo announcements.

In addition, we also have affordable advertising and a Must Read list – based on quality, ratings and sellable titles selected by our staff – that we promote on our social sites like Twitter and Facebook.

Please visit our site: http://kindlebookpromos.luckycinda.com

2. Digital Book Today – The site's owner, Anthony Wessel, is a retail industry book veteran of the 90's with Borders/Waldenbooks and re-entered the eBook industry in 2010. He works primarily with small press publishers and indie authors. His goal is to connect e-readers with e-authors. A special feature of his site is an exclusive top

100 list – based on quality, ratings and sellable titles selected by site staff - he advertises to ebook readers.

Digital Book Today also has free and paid advertising opportunities for authors. The prices are affordable and because of the site's following, it usually pays off to promote with Anthony.

Read more about Anthony:
http://galemartin.squarespace.com/blog/2012/6/26/meet-anthony-wessel-the-man-behind-digital-book-today.html

Or go to the site: http://digitalbooktoday.com/

3. GoodReads – This is an author-friendly website with an expansive collection of groups consisting of book reviewers, readers and authors. The groups are engaged, interactive and responsive. If you're an author, membership is FREE. Authors also get a page to post books, photos and promotions.

Once you've joined, search for "book reviewers," "book clubs," and "bloggers seeking authors." You can send messages to the administrators of each group or you can post at the threads in the forums.

GoodReads also offers Pay Per Click advertising similar to Google's, except that the people looking at ads on this site actually want to buy books.

Please read the site's guidelines:
http://www.goodreads.com/

There are hundreds of other sites helpful to authors. Each provides lists that help navigation into territories featuring author promotion. Many of these sites offer services for improving your writing, or your product's ultimate package.

Here are a few sites we have used and have found helpful:

http://authormarketingclub.com/ - Many free author tools

http://parapub.com/sites/para/ - You can list your titles here for free and the site has reviewers too

http://thewritingbomb.blogspot.com/

http://www.thecreativepenn.com/

http://www.thebookdesigner.com/

http://jakonrath.blogspot.com/

http://hauntedcomputer.blogspot.com/p/kindle-tour-stops.html

Top Book Marketing GURUS

Patricia Fry - http://www.patriciafry.com/

Brian Jud - http://www.bookmarketingworks.com/

John Kremer - http://www.bookmarket.com/

Dan Poynter - http://parapub.com/sites/para/

Book sites with author tools and advertising possibilities

Digital Book Today - http://digitalbooktoday.com/

World Literary Café - http://worldliterarycafe.com/

The Kindle Book Review -
http://thekindlebookreview.blogspot.com/

PRICE POINTS: Manipulating ebook prices for better sales:
Trial and error is the only surefire method of determining the
appropriate price for any Kindle ebook. Many authors charge $5 or
less, until they start achieving consistent sales.
Price points depend so much on your categories, genre and previous
sales.

For instance, immediately prior to our first promotion for *Francesca
of Lost Nation*, we set our digital book at $9.99. Although we didn't
alter that price for a day, we still sold downloads. An additional 23
were borrowed through the Lending Library.

Two days after our promotion, we dropped the price to .99 cents and
yet made far fewer sales. So what went wrong?

a. We should have retained the $9.99 until our rankings began dropping. By making a change mid-stream, as it were, we interrupted the book's momentum and ran afoul of Amazon algorithms.

b. It's difficult to say whether pricing the book at .99 cents to begin with could have resulted in more sales. On our second promotion we priced the book at $3.99 and made nearly $300.

Some authors have made a killing with their .99 cent books. Perhaps the most famous Amazon self-publisher is John Locke, a New York Times best-selling author and an international best-selling author of 11 books in three distinct genres.

According to his Amazon profile, Locke is the 8th author in history to have sold one million ebooks on Kindle and the first self-published author in history to have done so.

He currently offers some Kindle titles at $2.99 – which, by the way, seems to be the accepted norm. If you have a really fine product, you can charge $4.99 and higher, especially if your work fills a sought-after specialty niche and the book has little competition.

Think OUTSIDE the Box:

Try offering a sweetener to entice readers back to your book, once your Amazon ranking start to slide.

Author Cheryl Kaye Tardif, made $42,000 in one month using the KDP plan she outlined in her book, *How I made $42,000 in 1 month Selling My Kindle ebooks.*

She suggests hosting a Twitter party during which you offer prizes and drawings to book purchasers. You could also make yourself available to chat and respond to questions for at least 30 minutes as a special bonus.

Tardiff also recommends hosting Facebook contests using site www.rafflecopter.com to help with arrangements and giveaways.

Author Phil Torcivia of *Fifty Shades of Silver Hair and Socks* offers fellow authors 30 day free postings of their Kindle titles on his site: http://thekindledailydeal.com/bargains.cfm which claims 15,000 subscribers. While purchase of his book isn't required, he does request those who list their titles to buy.

Is this author sneaky or a marketing genius? Wish we'd thought of it! Not only did he find a way to pile onto the popularity of the "*Fifty Shades of Gray*" series through parody but he makes additional sales with a much-sought after author service.

We think sweeteners are such a powerful strategy, we're providing a BONUS CHAPTER for this book!

Chapter 9 – Bonus Chapter: How to make even more $$$ with Kindle and digital titles

Many authors focus on KDP – select free promos and forget there are other ways to capitalize on Amazon. We have outlined four possibilities for you:

Section I - KDP Select Lending Library:

Writers can earn royalties through Amazon's Lending Library, an option available to anyone enrolling in the KDP Select program.

The Lending Library is a service available exclusively to Kindle Prime Members who pay an annual fee for the privilege of "borrowing" one book per month for free. Amazon provides a monthly KDP Select Fund – $600,000 for the month of July, 2012 – which is shared among KDP authors.

So, along with any books you sold through KDP, you would also receive a royalty payment for each copy of your enrolled titles "borrowed" by Prime Members. This amount might well be higher than your sales commissions ... yet another reason why we adore AMAZON.

The Lending Library allows you to keep promoting your book for FREE – at least to Prime Members. You can write blog posts, schedule weekly tweets and remind your email list and Facebook fans (who also happen to be Amazon Prime Members) that they can "check out" your book for FREE. Later on, if they choose to buy it, so much the better – you'll be making money twice!

Section II - Become a publishing mini-magnate - Offer multiple books:

The more books you publish through Kindle, the more sales you will generate. Since trilogies are hugely popular right now, if you have written a series, it will be easier to sell your second and third book to the fans who already enjoyed your original effort. (This is one instance where the reputation for excellence you have built over time will prove invaluable – not to mention lucrative.)

Of course, a series is not required. Simply enroll each of your titles in the KDP Select plan and promote each separately. By keeping the buzz going from book to book, you will create what marketers often refer to as "echo effect," that can boosts sales exponentially. By comparing and contrasting the overall response to your various products, you can determine which is the most successful and which needs a "facelift."

What you choose to publish, and how well you market what you publish, will determine your ultimate success. But there are dozens of authors who have used this program to create honest-to-goodness best sellers. There's no reason you can't do it for yourself.

Example One: Amanda Hocking published two books on Kindle between March and April of 2011, after a boatload of traditional publishers refused them. At her blog, http://amandahocking.blogspot.com, Hockings tells readers how she went from obscure nobody to bestseller.

Her books, *My Blood Approves* and *Fate,* only sold a combined total of 45 in two weeks. She decided to publish a third book, *Flutter* at the end of May 2011 – by June her total combined sales were 624 units.

Hocking realized the more books she had available, the greater her sales. She also discovered where to get help for free publicity: Book Bloggers.

By July, Hocking had sold over 3,500 books and earned over $6,000. She published yet another installation in her vampire series near the end of 2011 and was clearing more moolah than she was at her full-time day job. In addition to Amazon, the author credits her book bloggers who helped get the word out about her books.

Example two: Novelist J.A. Konrath has sold over 100,000 ebooks. At the end of 2010 he was selling 1,000 ebooks a DAY. On his blog, http://jakonrath.blogspot.com, Konrath recommends authors keep their book price under $3 and emphasizes quality content and a great cover. (Sound familiar?)

Isn't it time you added your name to the BESTSELLERS list?

Section III - Kindle Singles:

Amazon offers an interesting and relatively unknown platform called Kindle Singles. Kindle Singles (KS) are short stories, novellas or long-from essays intended to be read in one sitting.

To participate in KS, authors should submit a pitch to kindle-singles@amazon.com with a description of the content. Please visit the site for more detailed info.

We also recommend you purchase one or two in the categories that interest you to become familiar with what type of content Amazon may be seeking.

How to be considered: If your work is already available through KDP, Amazon will also need the ASIN of your Kindle Store title and your KDP account email address. If you haven't yet published the manuscript in question, you can include it along with your submission query.

Sometimes Amazon pays an advance for a Kindle Single piece; sometimes it pays royalties. As we write this, there's little competition on this site, so a high KS category ranking is reasonably attainable even for new writers.

Kindle Singles is a real showcasing opportunity for underemployed journalists and freelance magazine writers or new-timers dipping their toes into written word-associated communication. It offers free expression of ideas; subjects and opinions that are well researched and presented; and a way to publically distribute material that would probably otherwise never see the light of day.

Of course, publishing houses and media outlets have to be selective in what they distribute which is why so many interesting, well-written stories get lost in the shuffle. Through Amazon Kindle Singles, any good writer can get noticed – and paid!

Potential KS revenue: In March of 2012, an outfit called PaidContent interviewed a dozen writers regarding their sales figures on Kindle Singles. While the actual revenue varied widely, one writer topped six-figures and another estimated his take at around $8,000.

Section IV - Provide other Kindle authors publicity:

The popularity of the KDP Select program has flooded book sites designed primarily to spread the word about FREE PROMOTIONS. It's reached a point where many websites are already sold out of pre-paid pre-holiday ad space.

You may be interested in making money promoting other authors over, or in addition to, writing and promoting your own work.

Here is a simple plan of action:

- Set up a blog where authors can promote their FREE days and make money through the Amazon Advantage plan. When you sign on as an affiliate, you'll make a percentage from every book sale originated from your website

- Offer ad packages for authors seeking to promote their titles

- Team with other websites to increase your links, followers, fans and sales
- Build your email list from the visitors and users of your site

- Sell your own books by including them in the price of your advertisement and/or give them to new customers as an incentive. You could also offer free services in exchange for a book sale

Chapter 10 – Final Thoughts

We believe that every reader of every book, whatever the topic or genre, deserves the utmost respect and heartfelt thanks of the writer. We appreciate the time, energy and financial investment YOU have made to get HERE. We also know how difficult marketing a book can be in this age of computerized publishing and in light of the sheer volume of book publishing-related statistics.

We encourage you to continue in your writing pursuits, because frankly, this old world needs all the thoughtful, accomplished writers it can get.

We hope the material presented here has been helpful. If you have questions or comments, please don't hesitate to drop us a line at: **laura@luckycinda.com**.

We encourage you to purchase our other books:
Francesca of Lost Nation -
http://www.amazon.com/dp/B003MGKA5Y/

The Adventures of Baylard Bear: a story about being DIFFERENT –
http://www.amazon.com/dp/1470047470/

Please leave reviews on Amazon if you like any of our work. HERE's to YOUR SUCCESS. We wish you all the best.

About the authors

Lucinda Sue Crosby is an award-winning journalist and environmentalist as well as a published and recorded Nashville songwriter. She's also had a successful TV and film career, traveled the world as a professional athlete and worked as a sports color commentator for the Women's Tennis Association via InDemand Pay-Per-View.

NOTE: "The Author's Show" selected Lucinda Sue Crosby as a 2011 honoree in "50 Great Writers You Should be Reading." Crosby is also a **Kindle bestselling author** of two books, *Francesca of Lost Nation* and *The Adventures of Baylard Bear – a story about being DIFFERENT.* (Both books are award-winners)

Laura Dobbins is a former newspaper editor, award-winning journalist and page designer. She enjoys reading, going to movies and fishing.

Reach the authors: http://luckycinda.com/

Reference Page

Recommended Books:

The Indie Author's Guide Make a Killing on Kindle (Without Bloggin, Facebook or Twitter: The Guerilla Marketer's Guide to Selling Ebooks on Amazon) By Michael Alvear

50 ways to promote your ebook by Patricia Fry
FREE download: http://www.patriciafry.com

KDP SelectTM: Navigating Kindle's Freebie Day by Dan Poytner

How I made $42,000 in 1 month Selling My Kindle ebooks
By Cheryl Kaye Tardif

Recommended Blog Posts:

Lucinda Sue Crosby - "How to become a successful Wordsmith"
http://writingwell.luckycinda.com

Jessica Park – "How Amazon saved my Book"
http://indiereader.com/2012/06/how-amazon-saved-my-life/.

Author Hope – "how to place your book in the proper category"
http://digitalbooktoday.com/getting-your-ebook-in-the-proper-category-for-improved-ranking/

The Codex Group Study – Book buyer habits
http://www.thebookdoctors.com/does-an-author-really-need-a-website-the-book-doctors-interview-annik-lafarge-on-how-to-be-a-more-effective-author-online

Recommend Book Editors:

Elizabeth McAdams, Beaumont Hardy *Editing*
jane@beaumonthardy.com

Neal Hock
http://www.hockseditingservices.com/

Recommended Publishers:

Kindle Direct Publishing – Select (Has 90 day exclusive clause)
http://kdp.amazon.com

CreateSpace – Print on Demand
https://www.createspace.com/

Smashwords – Print on Demand and Digital
(No exclusive clause)
https://www.smashwords.com/

Wholesaler:
Lightning Source – Print on Demand, part of Ingram Group Content
: Lists your titles with Baker and Taylor, Amazon and Barnes and
Noble and makes your titles available to any bookstore worldwide
http://www1.lightningsource.com/

Book Design:

Createspace: http://www.createspace.com

The Small Publishers, Artists and Writers Network (SPAWN) offer a
$100 book design discount to its members for services at:
http://www.logicalexpressions.com/

John Kremer, book marketing expert and bestselling author, has an
extensive list of artists at his website:
http://www.bookmarket.com/101des.htm

Art and photo sites

Clip Art
http://www.clipart.com/en/?lid=s48OP9MQZ&pcrid=6378290319&
property=CA

Photos/Illustrations
http://www.dreamstime.com/

Photos/Art
http://www.flickr.com/creativecommons/

Free E-book conversion
http://ebook.online-convert.com/convert-to-epub

http://www.epubconverter.org/

Recommended FREE books about e-book conversion:

1. *Building Your Book for Kindle* by KDP
http://www.amazon.com/dp/B007URVZJ6/

2. *Building Your Book for Kindle for MAC* by KDP
http://www.amazon.com/dp/B00822K3Z0/

3. *Smashwords Style Guide – How to Format Your Ebook*
(Smashwords Guide) by Mark Coker
http://www.amazon.com/dp/B004XWJ7UK/

Web Hosts:
http://www.hostgator.com
http://www.webhostingchoice.com

Other author tools:

Author Joanna Penn offers a copy of her Award-winning marketing
plan as a free download on her website:
http://www.thecreativepenn.com/2009/02/20/award-winning-marketing-plan/

Dan Poynter – "Book Cover Worksheet" Free download
http://parapub.com/sites/para/resources/allproducts.cfm

Step by Step Self-Publishing Blog
http://www.stepbystepselfpublishing.net/reviewer-list.html

Book Marketing and Book Promotion
http://www.bookmarket.com/magazines-books.htm

Book Reviews:

Amazon
http://www.amazon.com/review/top-reviewers

The Midwest Book Review
http://www.midwestbookreview.com/index.html

GoodReads
http://www.goodreads.com/

The Book Blogger Directory
http://bookbloggerdirectory.wordpress.com/

Author Interviews
http://kindlebookpromos/luckycinda.com

http://www.facebook.com/dailynews22
(KindleBookPromos)

Here are a few sites we have used and have found helpful:
(as we listed earlier in the book)

http://authormarketingclub.com/ - Many free author tools

http://parapub.com/sites/para/ - You can list your titles here for free
and the site has reviewers too

http://thewritingbomb.blogspot.com/

http://www.thecreativepenn.com/

http://www.thebookdesigner.com/

http://jakonrath.blogspot.com/

http://hauntedcomputer.blogspot.com/p/kindle-tour-stops.html

Top Book Marketing GURUS:

Patricia Fry - http://www.patriciafry.com/

Brian Jud - http://www.bookmarketingworks.com/

John Kremer - http://www.bookmarket.com/

Dan Poynter - http://parapub.com/sites/para/

Promotion Listing Sites:

http://kindlebookpromos.luckycinda.com

http://digitalbooktoday.com/

http://worldliterarycafe.com/

http://thekindlebookreview.blogspot.com/

http://thekindleromancereview.blogspot.com/

http://thewomensnest.com/content/social_media_mania_get_marketing_buzz_your_book

http://ebookswag.com/

http://kindlenationdaily.com/

http://www.centsibleereads.com/

http://www.99-cent-network.com/www.99-cent-Network.com/Home.html

http://www.independentauthornetwork.com/index.html

http://www.kindleboards.com/
http://blog.booksontheknob.org/p/about-this-blog-and-contact-info.html

http://addictedtoebooks.com/submission

http://authormarketingclub.com/members/submit-your-book/

http://bargainebookhunter.com/feature-your-book/

http://ereadernewstoday.com/ent-free-book-submissions/

http://www.freebooksy.com/

http://flurriesofwords.blogspot.com/

http://www.indiebookslist.com/kdp-select-submission-form/

http://www.mediabistro.com/appnewser/category/free-ebooks

http://www.pixelofink.com/sfkb/

http://snickslist.com/books/place-ad/

http://storyfinds.com/

http://www.ereaderiq.com/free/
Fill out the contact form

http://www.fkbooksandtips.com/
Send email to Michael Gallagher – kindle@gagler.com

http://cheapkindledaily.wordpress.com/

http://thefrugalereader.wufoo.com/forms/frugal-freebie-submissions/

Facebook:

http://www.facebook.com/dailynews22
(KindleBookPromos)

http://www.facebook.com/allthingskindle
Site requires a five day advance notice contact –
stepartdesigns@hotmail.com

http://www.facebook.com/AontheC
http://www.facebook.com/authormarketingclub

http://www.facebook.com/BookGoodies

http://www.facebook.com/earthsbooknook

http://www.facebook.com/eReader1

http://www.facebook.com/freeebookdeal

http://www.facebook.com/fkbooksandtips

http://www.facebook.com/galleycat/app_4949752878

http://www.facebook.com/iauthor

http://www.facebook.com/IndieBookLounge

http://www.facebook.com/IndieKindleWLC

http://www.facebook.com/kindle

http://www.facebook.com/KindleFreebies

http://www.facebook.com/KindleKorner

http://www.facebook.com/kindledailydeal

http://www.facebook.com/readingkindle

http://www.facebook.com/TheKindleObsessed

http://www.facebook.com/weloveebooks

http://www.facebook.com/StoryFinds

http://www.facebook.com/BookLending

http://www.facebook.com/pages/UK-Kindle-Book-Lovers/175617412524192

http://www.facebook.com/groups/341840249197060

http://www.facebook.com/groups/UK.Kindle.Reading

Twitter:

@penabook
@4FreeKindleBook
@BookBub
@DigitalBKToday
@DigitalInkToday
@FreeReadFeed
@KindleFreeBook
@KindleBookKing
@kindleebooks
@TheLuvOfBooks
@Kindlestuff
@KindleEbooksUK
@fkbt
@FreeKindleDude
@FreeKindleBooks

@FreeReadFeed
@PixelofInk
@WLCauthor
@kindlenews

Retweet Teams:

http://worldliterarycafe.com/
Has twitter programs including RT teams.

http://www.booktweetingservice.com/
Offers paid RT programs.

Book sites with author tools and advertising possibilities

Digital Book Today - http://digitalbooktoday.com/

World Literary Café - http://worldliterarycafe.com/

The Kindle Book Review -
http://thekindlebookreview.blogspot.com/